GW01086468

Stop Your Teenager Stealing

Easy Steps to Stop the Stealing Today

Elizabeth O'Shea

Contents

Stop your Teenager Stealing
The Elizabeth O'Shea method

Introduction

Stealing in teenagers is common. Most children will take something that doesn't belong to them at some point. However, it's behaviour that you need to tackle, and stop.

Perhaps you have just discovered your teenager is stealing. Perhaps you have had an ongoing problem with things going missing in your home. Or perhaps you've tried to punish your teenager, but the stealing has continued. This guide will help in all of these situations, and give you some useful insights to tackle the stealing effectively and put a stop to it.

Often teenagers who steal regularly secretly feel annoyed about something that's happening at home. Perhaps they feel invisible, or feel entitled to money or things. Your teenager may not understand 'why' they steal. However, most teenagers don't like themselves very much for stealing. They may want to change but don't know *how*. Taking things becomes a habit.

No teenager wants to get caught. At first, when they realise the stealing has been discovered, they may be distraught. Or try to make light of it. Or they may be angry and defiant. However, if you handle it in the right way, you can help your teenager to take responsibility for what they've done and learn not to steal again.

This guide describes the Elizabeth O'Shea method for tackling stealing. It contains many useful hints and tips you can use. The guide is compact. So I would recommend you read it all before having that crucial conversation about stealing with your teenager. It's useful to understand how your teenager may be thinking. And practicing your responses means you will be fully prepared to handle the conversation in the best possible way depending on how your teenager reacts, and what you discover. Every situation (where a teenager steals) is different, so you will need to adapt the conversation you have to *your* teenager and what they have taken.

The first section of this guide looks at why teenagers steal and gives you points to consider when confronting a teenager.
Part 1 looks at 10 ways to prepare before you confront your teenager.
Part 2 describes how to actually have the conversation with your teenager. And provides you with some sample phrases and conversations.
Part 3 explores how to repair the relationship with your teenager.
And finally there are suggestions on what to do if the stealing continues.

If you suspect your teenager is stealing but don't have any evidence

You need to become a detective. It's so much easier to confront your teenager with evidence.

If you have more than one child, find out which child is spending more than usual.

Your teenager won't like the thought of having their room searched. But if you have a good reason to suspect that they may have taken your belongings, they have already broken your trust. You have a responsibility to your teenager to stop behaviour that could result in a criminal record. And privacy is earned, it's not a right.

If you choose to search your teenager's room, common hiding places are the pockets of old clothes, under the mattress, under the bed, the back of a wardrobe or drawer, or a 'secret' hiding place (think where that could be for your teenager). If your teenager is really determined for you not to find something they've stolen they may use a hollowed-out book, or tape what they've stolen behind drawers.

Mark any bank notes in your purse so if your teenager takes them you will know they were from your purse (but don't leave money lying around, because that's just putting temptation in your teenager's way. And it isn't OK to deliberately try to catch them out).

Confronting your teenager

If you have only just discovered your teenager is stealing, you are probably feeling overwhelmed and upset. You may want to confront your child at the earliest opportunity.

Please wait until you've read this guide, and worked out exactly what you want to say.

Confronting your teenager in the right way is vital. It may feel urgent that you have the conversation as soon as your teenager walks through the door. But it is better to plan the conversation so you say and do the right things. At the end of the conversation it's important to maintain your relationship with your teenager, and for your teenager to feel sorry and remorseful. That takes careful thought and planning.

As I've just mentioned, if you just suspect your teenager has been stealing, and have no evidence, then I would strongly suggest you get some evidence before you confront them. If there is the shadow of a doubt, it's unlikely your teenager will confess to stealing. And in the future, your teenager will be more careful about hiding any thing they've stolen.

In a while I'm going to go through a script. The actual words you can use to challenge your teenager over the stealing, so that your teenager realises the impact of what they've done and will hopefully stop stealing in the future. But first, we're going to look at how you can understand your teenager, and prepare to confront them.

This is a conversation they'll look back on in future years - the day they got caught. So it's important to say the right things and help them remember it for the RIGHT reasons

A word of warning
This is the moment you have the opportunity to stop your teenager stealing.

If you let your teenager get off too lightly – you won't stop them, the stealing will continue. If it continues, there is a possibility your teenager could lose friends, respect from other people, and possibly end up with a criminal record. This could affect their career prospects for the rest of their life.

It's important to remember you are not responsible for the poor choices your teenager makes. If, sometime in the future, your teenager gets arrested for stealing, gets a criminal record or if they end up spending time in prison for theft, it will be their own actions that have caused it.

However, today you have the chance to stop the stealing. If you can do that, you will be doing your son or daughter a big favour. And make it less likely that stealing will cause them to lose friends, lose respect from others, or possibly get them into trouble with the law. But you need to handle the situation really well to stop your teenager now.

If you are too severe – your teenager will hate you – they'll rebel against you – and they will go further down the path of being determined to defy you. If you punish your teenager with arbitrary consequences you may lose their respect and the relationship between you will deteriorate. It may take many years for your teenager to feel close to you again. And sometimes, it may not be possible to repair the damage.

If you can give sufficient *appropriate* consequences for the stealing – you may be able to stop it. The consequences I'm going to ask you to give will hopefully help your teenager regain their belief in their own self-worth, regain their respect for you, understand how their stealing has affected the people around them, and stop them feeling entitled to take other people's possessions.

It is also important to let your teenager know what consequences they will be *choosing* if they ever steal anything again. Your ultimate aim should be to stop the stealing habit and get through this, with your relationship intact so you can continue to influence your teenager for the better.

Stealing from the perspective of a teenager

Your teenager probably won't think of themselves as a bad person. No one does. They may have no idea why they're taking things. It's just a habit they have.

Your teenager may justify the theft of things at home as a consequence for something either you or one of your children has done to them. Perhaps not appreciating them or giving them the attention or respect they feel they deserve.

If your teenager has been stealing from shops or from friends, they may well have convinced themselves that it isn't fair that they don't have the money for the things other people can afford. They have the same right to have nice things. Or they may think the shops are making a fortune and can afford it.

They may have convinced themselves that stealing isn't so bad. They may have friends who steal regularly and get away with it. And who boast about the things they've stolen. They may even be admired for it!

Or it could be the thrill. The adrenaline rush they get from doing something dangerous.

All teenagers think that they're good kids. And sometimes they just want to rebel and do something no one would expect them to do – in order to show they're independent. They *may* do other things too - it might be looking at porn sites, smoking, drinking alcohol, taking drugs or possibly having sex without you knowing. They may think that stealing is no big deal. As long as you don't find out.

Deep down though, they're probably not very proud of themselves for stealing. Taking things has become a habit. They know it's wrong. They worry about being caught, and they may want to stop but don't know how.

How might your teenager behave if they're caught?

Your teenager may just want to avoid the consequences. And lie or do anything to avoid getting the blame. If they're stealing their moral compass has gone off-course, and they probably don't want to admit to it or take responsibility.

Besides, your teenager may have convinced themselves that you *almost* deserve it for being so naïve or trusting.

They will probably rely on you believing their story in order to get away with it. And may want to make you feel guilty for suspecting them in the first place.

And they'll be desperate to hide the full extent of their stealing. They won't want to own up to the number of things they've stolen in the past.

Once your teenager realises that the game is up, when they can't explain your evidence, and you don't believe their excuse or story… Your teenager may get angry, or upset, or both. Being caught may feel like the worst thing that has ever happened to them.

Your teenager would not want to be demonised as a person, even if they had done something wrong. They would desperately want to keep their reputation intact. And not be seen as a thief.

Your teenager would want the consequences to be fair – and related to what they did – rather than severe and arbitrary. They might not like the consequences you suggest, but they'd want to understand why they were being imposed.

Once they realise how it has affected you, and damaged the trust between you, they should want to earn that trust back.

The most effective way to confront your teenager about stealing.

Years later, your teenager will probably realise it was good they were caught. The stealing was a habit that could have resulted in a criminal conviction. Right now they probably don't feel very good about stealing. But they don't know how to stop.

In the future, your teenager may still get an occasional urge to take something that doesn't belong to them – but they'll appreciate that if they really want something they'll have to earn it. And they'll be much more aware of what the consequences could be – and how embarrassing it could be if they ever stole something and got caught.

If you confront your teenager effectively, your teenager will eventually feel closer to you. And sorry they ever took things from you. It's hard to believe now, but if you handle the situation well, you may even end up closer to your teenager than you were before you discovered the stealing.

Parents' stories

Sometimes when you're worried about stealing you can feel so alone. It's useful to hear other parents' stories so that you know you're not the only one, and that other parents are struggling with exactly the same issues.

There is a blog on the Parent 4 Success website: **'41 things you can do if your teenager steals from you'**, where parents have chosen to share their stories about teenagers stealing. Here are a few examples of the messages parents have posted:

Brian:
My 13 year old daughter has been caught taking money from my wife and me, a bit here and there over a 2 month period which added up to nearly £30.00. I did not want to jump into this without thinking first, and this article was a tremendous help. It has shown me that there are other issues (that we are aware of) that contributed to why she has done this. I now know how to handle the situation confidently, will help her to sort these issues and this should prevent an escalation of the problem.

Andrea:
Hi, My 14 year old son is stealing money from us. Just recently he took nearly $200 from my bank account. This comes after he just got in trouble for being disrespectful to me and his stepdad. He said he used part of it on a gift card, which he claims he lost the same day, and the other part on food for his "friends". I really do not know what to do. In the past, a few years ago, I had issues with him taking things that did not belong to him. I suppose he never really stopped? I really do not know what to do. I'm at my wits' end with him – and just feel like giving up. I cannot trust him at all. He seems to not only steal, but

lie about everything. When you talk to him he's very logical and rational about it, which worries me even more.

Steve:

I really didn't realise that my 17 year old son was capable of doing what he did and that was to steal an iPad from his sister and to delete the data and give to his girlfriend for a present. I was mortified and totally gutted and dealt with it in a lot of these ways. I will use some more of the items in the list now I have read the article and hopefully he will not re-offend. Thanks.

Niki:

Hi

Thank you for the article, I am going through this at the moment, I have 3 children so not entirely sure which one it is, but I do suspect one above the others. I have tried grounding, removing electronic devices and letting them know how disappointed I am on earlier occasions, have also taken to locking our money away but then last night £5 was stolen again.

I will print this article out and go through the points with them, I do need to get to the bottom of why this is happening as it is coming between my partner and me, who is stepdad to the two eldest children.

Lanay:

My 18 year old son is a senior in High School this year. This past summer, he refused to get a job, and he just wanted to hang out with his friends. He never asked me for money, did the odd lawn mowing job, and I was a fool, I believed him. Here he was taking money from my bank account bit by bit until $1500 was missing and a check I wrote bounced. I confronted him, he said he blew most of it on gas, liquor and pot.

I am such a fool. He was basically under house arrest from August until just a couple weeks ago. I took his car and told him he couldn't have one of my vehicles again until he could pass a drug test cleanly and had a job to start paying me back. I relaxed house arrest a couple of weeks ago, he has applications in at several businesses but I haven't given a vehicle back. He told me recently he couldn't pass a clean test. My next stipulation was to see a therapist. He was very upset, saying people can't get addicted to pot and even more scary, how pot helped him with his homework and helped him sleep.

I'm at my wits' end, wondering where he got the money to pay for this pot he has been smoking; he says a friend gives it to him on occasion (which I do not believe).

Tonight I found my heirloom pearls missing. These pearls and bracelet are irreplaceable and passed on to me by my mother before she died 20 years ago. I know he has taken them. I don't want to think so, I want to be wrong. But I cannot find them anywhere. I went to look for them after I was told by a family member my son was trying to pawn the watch his grandfather had given him and now I am sick to my stomach that this is where my mom's pearls have gone.

How do I even start this conversation without bawling? Where do I go if he denies the theft? I hate that my first thought upon missing my pearls is that my son has taken them. The pearls might be irreplaceable but my son is even more so and he is heading down this path of destruction.

Julie:

My daughter was 15 (now 16) when she stole several things from me. I found a dish from my closet in her room that had contained money. I found a coin purse from my closet that contained money, in her room, empty. I found my coin collection under her bed. I have no way of knowing how much money is gone, or if all the coins are still there. In addition, she stole a bottle of Vicodin. I am pretty sure there are other items that I didn't realize were gone. She lied many times before she was finally forced to admit she had taken it (she admitted it in therapy only). She does not accept my rationale. She shows no remorse.

Perhaps you can relate to these stories, or maybe your situation is completely different. Regardless of what your teenager has stolen, this guide will help.

Why do teenagers steal?

Many teenagers have no idea why they steal. They imagine it's because they want something that belongs to someone else. But it's rarely as simple as that. So it's useful to look at what *may* be going on for your teenager.

Sometimes your teenager *may* just want what someone else has got. And feel they should have good things just as much as anyone else. They may not think before they take it. There are two underlying causes: poor self-control *and* a sense of entitlement.

'Entitlement' could be a big factor in your teenager taking things. Your teenager may secretly feel that they are not treated as well as they would like. Perhaps they feel they 'deserve' good things. They might believe that they are entitled to receive things that they don't have to earn. This could be because you, as parents, try to do everything around the home, and don't expect your teenagers to help. Your teenager may have learned to *expect* good things without doing anything to deserve them. Effectively you may have 'trained' your teenager to expect you to do everything, because you have always done it!

It's possible your teenager may be stealing because they feel distant from you, from members of the family or other teenagers at school. They may feel alone, different, disconnected, unloved, unappreciated or just that they don't 'belong'. They may think they have a right to hurt other people because they feel unhappy inside. In a way the 'stealing' may be trying to make up for the pain they feel in what can be seen as an attempt to 'get even.' Feeling distant from other people can mean your teenager doesn't feel enough empathy towards others. (It is important to make sure that if your teenager is stealing, afterwards you go to extra lengths to help them feel loved, important and wanted.)

Perhaps your teenager wants to think of themselves as 'bad.' It becomes a badge of honour to be dominating and nasty. The stealing can be an extension of the need to identify with the 'bad boys or girls' and shock others into realising they have a tough, mean side. Sometimes they are shocked at their own 'nastiness'. And don't understand why they are behaving that way. They don't understand that it's human nature to test boundaries and explore different behaviours.

It *could* be that your teenager is stealing because they don't have a 'firm but fair' parent; because you, as parents, aren't in charge at home; because you don't know how to discipline your teenager when they behave badly; or because you haven't had the confidence or authority to get your teenager to help out at home and contribute to family life.

Your teenager may want attention. They may be stealing as a sort of 'cry for help', in order to feel important, and enjoy the mayhem and disruption that comes from things going missing in the family home.

It could be they are jealous of a sibling– if your teenager feels a brother or sister is the 'favourite,' or gets more positive attention or praise. Perhaps you praise a sibling for being more intelligent, hard working or superior in some way. Or you always treat a brother or sister as a victim, and don't notice the annoying things they do to wind your teenager up. If this is the case it is useful to listen carefully to what your teenager says and look at what you could be doing to make sibling rivalry worse.

It may be because they want to pay for gifts for friends or family to gain acceptance and good-will. Of course it's easier to be generous with money they've stolen. But they may not actually know how to earn money they want to pay for presents.

Your teenager could be stealing because of peer pressure, or because they want to fit in with a group or gang where stealing is normal.

It could be to fund a habit such as gambling, on-line gaming or funding cigarettes or alcohol.

In a good proportion of situations teenagers may steal to fund buying pot /cannabis or other drugs. Although you may dismiss this in your own teenager's case, please don't rule this out as a possibility. Just be vigilant and ready for this. If your teenager confesses to taking drugs when you talk to them, you should thank your teenager for being honest, tell your teenager you need to think about that one, and that you'll help get it sorted, but you'll need to come back to them when you've worked out the best way to tackle it. Then do your research or get some professional advice.

Your teenager could be stealing because they don't want to feel dependent on anyone. They take what they need so they don't have to ask for money or feel obliged to anyone – particularly if they are hostile or resentful towards you.

They may be angry over an argument or feel upset about the way they've been treated by another teenager at school. And they might want to get their own back.

Or they may just feel jealous of another teenager. And take their things just because they don't feel it's 'fair' that something in another person's life seems better than their own.

And it has to be considered that they could be stealing due to demands from a bully.

No matter why your teenager has stolen, it's important that they repay the money or replace the goods and make up for the hurt they caused if you want to stop them stealing again. They must recognise there will be some long term work to do to repair the relationship.

If you don't know HOW to get your teenager to help at home, deal with sibling rivalry or re-build a relationship contact me or find a parenting specialist to help. Stealing is just a symptom that something is wrong. Investing in professional help can help you get back the family life you want, and help get things back on track for your teenager. You are not alone. There is help. There are solutions. Good parents seek help when they need it.

The effect stealing may have on you

When you first suspect your teenager of stealing, it can be devastating. Money may have gone missing, or you may have discovered items in your teenager's possession that you know they couldn't afford or suspect belonged to someone else.

It can lead to a whole range of emotions such as feeling hurt, let-down, shocked, disbelieving, sad, angry, upset, or disrespected.

In some ways, dealing with your teenager stealing can feel like a 'loss.' You may feel the image of your teenager as a 'good kid' has been ruined. Or you may feel that you've failed as a parent to instil the right morals into your teenager. You may feel that trust is essential in any relationship and that your connection with your teenager will never be the same again. Or you may be worried that your teenager may be arrested and charged with theft, which could affect their career prospects for life.

It's very important to take care of yourself during this difficult time. You need some adult support. Do you have a friend or relative you can talk to about this, who you know will keep your teenager's stealing confidential? Is there another person who can help you emotionally while you deal with your teenager's stealing habit?

Points to consider

Try to keep a sense of perspective. Most children steal at some point. Most teenagers who steal aren't 'bad kids', they've just made a mistake in judgement – a poor choice. With your help and support your teenager will regain a healthy self-esteem. And stop stealing.

Even if you think your teenager is going off the rails, and you don't think of them as a 'good kid', you need to help your teenager to believe that they are basically good. They may just be making some poor decisions at the moment. Trust that eventually your teenager will turn out ok. And keep that image in your head. If your teenager doesn't believe you have faith they can stop stealing, they won't have the confidence to do it themselves.

Your relationship with your teenager is more important than the items that went missing. But the breach in trust caused by the stealing will affect your relationship for a while. You do need to stop the stealing so your teenager learns not to take things that don't belong to them. You will need to be strong and completely firm about allowing your teenager to face the 'natural consequences' of their stealing.

In the short term, your teenager will almost certainly dislike you. Facing the consequences of their own actions is hard. And your teenager is going to struggle when you make them take responsibility for what they took. You need to keep in mind that your job as a parent is to help your teenager to become an adult with good morals. You may find it very hard to be disliked by your teenager for a while. But it's really important to be calm but firm about the consequences.

Stealing is often a sign of a rift in how close your teenager feels to you. And when you impose consequences, that sense of disconnection will get bigger. But you can – and must – rebuild your relationship.

The first time you talk to your teenager about stealing, I would recommend that just returning what they have stolen is enough. This is to help your teenager preserve their reputation as a good kid. If your teenager has taken things before, but you haven't warned them of the consequences, I would suggest you treat this as your first conversation.

However, it's important to explain that if they steal *again*, they'll need to return what they stole AND apologise or own up to the person they've stolen from (which may be you of course!). This isn't to humiliate your teenager but to help them take responsibility for their actions. Make sure your teenager is in no doubt that if there ever is a next time, this is the consequence they will be choosing. They will have made the conscious decision to steal, knowing that they will have to admit that they've taken something to the person they've stolen from. Your teenager needs to believe that you will be firm and enforce this.

Try to preserve your teenager's good reputation by *not* talking to friends and relatives about the stealing. The exception to this is your partner, or a relative or friend who can support you and who you *know* will keep your teenager's stealing habit confidential. Respect your teenager's right to a good reputation in the same way you wouldn't want other people gossiping about your mistakes in public.

Keep your money safely out of sight. And any other valuables that will tempt your teenager. It's common sense to keep temptation out of your teenager's way.

The difference between punishments and natural consequences

Punishments

Punishments are arbitrary, and have nothing to do with the 'crime': like confiscating a mobile phone, stopping your teenager going to a regular activity he or she loves, or grounding them for two weeks.

Initially, punishments may appear to work. But punishments will lead to more resentment and anger towards you, and they take away from your teenager's sense of shame or guilt, because your teenager feels almost justified in 'defying' your unjust power over them. As stealing is a symptom of a rift in your relationship, if your teenager feels annoyed and resentful about the punishments, the stealing (*and* other behaviours to defy you) may become more entrenched.

Ultimately, you want to regain a good relationship with your teenager, because your best hope of your teenager not stealing again is that they don't want to let you down. And a good, strong healthy relationship with your teenager is vital if your teenager is to stop stealing.

Natural consequences

Natural consequences are directly related to the stealing. And feel more 'reasonable.' Like earning money to pay back money that was stolen, returning items to shops or friends or relatives. Or doing jobs alongside a parent to make amends and rebuild trust.

Natural consequences are *harder* for your teenager, because they involve taking responsibility and making amends for the things they stole. However, they seem more justifiable as it seems relevant to return or pay back for items they've taken. It is important your teenager knows that if they're ever caught again, they will be *choosing* the consequence of apologising and owning up to the person they took things from. Having to own up to stealing is hard.

Hopefully your teenager will not want to lose face and risk stealing again.

The natural consequences of stealing the <u>first</u> time you confront your teenager

- Every item that was stolen needs to be returned.
- Any item that has been lost or broken needs to be paid for, and the cost of the item paid to the 'victim'.
- Any money stolen needs to be repaid. If this can be done anonymously, then that is OK – the first time.
- If your teenager doesn't still have the money in their possession, they must earn the money by doing jobs at home, at a rate of pay below the 'minimum wage', or find ways to earn the money.
  Even if the amount would equate to your teenager doing jobs for an hour a day for an entire year.
  If the money comes to a large amount, your teenager can choose to take half of the amount out of their savings account (if they have enough) and earn the rest.
- Your teenager should do 10-15 hours of jobs around the house, for free, to make up for the stress and upset the stealing has caused you.

Then you explain the consequences your teenager will be choosing (below) if they ever decide to steal again.

The natural consequences to your teenager of stealing a <u>second or subsequent</u> time:

- Your teenager should return anything they've taken, (or do jobs or paid work to return the equivalent value in money).
- They will need to own up and apologise to the person they took it from.
- They should do 15 hours of jobs at home – with no payment – to make amends for the hurt and loss of trust.
- A police officer will talk to them about the stealing.

The importance of being empathetic with your teenager

Empathy is:

- Being aware of the feelings and emotions of others, and experiencing them for ourselves through the power of imagination.
- When you place yourself in someone else's shoes and feel what they are feeling.

It's important to show that you 'understand' the strong emotions your teenager may be feeling when they get caught. Recognise the hard time they're having when they are confronted. It helps if your teenager can preserve a good opinion of themselves, despite what they've done. You can explain to your teenager:

"I know you're a 'good kid'. And just at the moment you seem to have lost your moral compass. But I'm going to help you get it back!"

Empathy is so important when it comes to relationships. Your teenager doesn't need battles, punishment and humiliation, they need understanding and empathy. This may not be what you're used to. And you may well be thinking of a suitable punishment for your teenager, because that's the way you've managed poor behaviour in the past.

If stealing is a side effect of a teenager who feels distant and disconnected, punishment isn't going to help. On the other hand, empathy might.

You are probably feeling (justifiably) very angry with your teenager for stealing. However, what do you really want to happen now?

You probably want your teenager to make amends, learn the lesson and never steal again. But if your teenager is going to learn the lesson it is vital that you reconnect with them.

Please don't mistake 'connecting with your teenager' as being 'soft.' There is nothing soft about helping a teenager learn through natural consequences. Apologising and earning the money to pay back for items that have been taken is not soft. It's very hard to do.

However, rather than treating 'natural consequences' as a punishment, you can explain why your teenager needs to face the consequences of stealing to help them learn, and stand by your teenager, whist still insisting they do the right thing. Stay completely calm when your teenager gets angry. Say *"I can see you're angry. I get this is hard."* And then don't say anything else. Just empathise with them and stay quiet.

Reconnecting with your teenager is about being kind. And showing unconditional love, while at the same time staying firm. Random punishments rarely work, but allowing a teenager to experience the natural consequences, while you are empathetic and by their side, is much more effective.

Talking to your teenager effectively about stealing has three parts.
Part 1 is preparation before you talk to your teenager.
Part 2 is the actual conversation.
Part 3 is repairing the relationship with your teenager afterwards.

Part 1:

10 ways to prepare for the conversation before confronting your teenager.

The following ten points need to be considered *before* you talk with your teenager. You may like to practise some of the responses so that you're prepared for the different ways in which your teenager may react. I've included some 'scripts' to illustrate what you could say. You can adapt what you say to the situation you're in.

You'll be ready to have the conversation when you feel confident that you can handle the situation calmly and know how to respond to your teenager well. It is better to delay the conversation if you don't feel ready. It's good to plan what you want to say, and plan when and where and how you'll say it to make sure that the impact of the conversation has the effect you want.

Let's assume, to start with, that £40 has gone missing from your purse, and you've found £40 under your teenager's mattress. We will look at how to deal with shoplifting later.

1. **The most important thing to remember: STAY COMPLETELY CALM**.
When dealing with your teenager's stealing, plan to stay calm and keep your voice low. 'Shouting' can be seen as a punishment. If you can maintain your self-control and stay calm and rational your teenager is less likely to get angry. They are forced to accept that you are being firm and reasonable when you insist they follow through with the natural consequences. They won't like taking responsibility, but they will find it easier if you don't lose your temper without distracting them from the true focus of attention – the stealing.

While you're talking to your teenager, do not lose your temper or get angry yourself. Keep your voice calm, confident and clear and make eye contact during your discussion. This is even the case if your teenager is adamant that they haven't taken it, or

> **The most important thing to remember: STAY COMPLETELY CALM.**

have no idea about how the money got into their room, or if your teenager becomes arrogant and nasty, and tells you they stole because you deserved it for some reason. It is really important that if you feel tempted to shout or feel yourself getting angry *leave the room* and say; *"I just need a bit of time to think. I'll be back in a few minutes."* Once you lose your temper the focus of attention moves from your teenager to you. And you'll have lost the moral high ground. So make sure you stay calm and in control while you confront your teenager.

2. Do you know exactly what happened? Do you have proof?

Could there be any other reason your teenager has this money in their possession? Do you need to speak to your partner or anyone else to check?

3. Can you plan to have the conversation in private?

Be careful not to embarrass your teenager by confronting them when brothers or sisters or other people can hear.

4. What will you say to start the conversation?

"I need to talk to you about something serious, is now a good time? If not, when can we talk today?"

5. Plan to describe the situation factually. Confront them with the evidence and don't accept excuses.

Put whatever you have found on the table in front of them.

"£40 went missing from my purse, and I decided to search the house, and I found this £40 under your mattress."

6. Try not to keep using the words 'stealing' or 'thief'.

It's OK to explain that what your teenager did was 'stealing.' However, don't labour the point and keep using the words 'stealing', 'thieving' or 'thief.' These words are very emotive and judgemental, and can make it less likely that your teenager will feel remorseful, rather than more likely. When people feel accused and judged, they find it hard to accept responsibility for doing something wrong. When they feel understood, they are more likely to want to make amends and repair the damage.

Instead, talk about 'taking things without asking', 'taking something that doesn't belong to them', 'making a mistake', 'an error of judgement', or a 'poor choice'. If you label your teenager as a thief, they may gradually live up to that reputation. The message you want your teenager to get is that they're a good kid who has done something out of character. It helps them feel more able to overcome this habit because you've let them preserve their self-esteem and their good opinion of themselves.

7. What will be the *best way* to approach the conversation to get what you want?

Do not ask your teenager *if* they stole the money if you already know they did. State that you *know* they took the item / money without asking. Do not get distracted from sorting this out if your teenager cries or gets angry. And do not imply at any time that you believe the excuses they might give. It's important that you take the stance that they have taken the item or money without asking. Don't go down the route of 'pretending' you believe their story at any time. If they deny taking the item or money, or try to give a plausible explanation, say you will be checking it out.

8. Think about what you want at the end of this conversation. What would be the best outcome?

When you decide on what you want out of the conversation, it makes it easier to plan what to say.

You probably want your teenager to admit that they made a mistake, make amends for what they took and not to take things that don't belong to them again.

Although you almost certainly want to have a good relationship with your teenager at the end, you need to be OK with the fact that your teenager is not going to like you for a while. Your teenager's future honesty rests on the consistency of your actions, and on how firm you are about insisting that they return anything they've stolen, or that they earn the money to pay for anything they've taken.

You probably want your teenager to know that you still love them, but that you're upset and disappointed in them, and never expected this from them.

You may also want to find out why they stole, and address any underlying problems.

Ultimately, you probably want to allow your teenager the chance to redeem themselves, and re-build your relationship and the trust you have in them.

9. Decide what messages you want to give your teenager.
Stealing is often a symptom that there is a rift in your relationship with your teenager. Although your first reaction may be to think of how you'll shame and punish your teenager, at the end of this conversation it would be good if your teenager feels a healthy 'guilt' about what they've done and is keen to repair the damage. Ultimately, they should want to rebuild their relationship with you so that they don't continue stealing, because it would let you down, and they would let themselves down.

The more time you spend going through and practising saying these messages aloud, the more likely it is that they will come out naturally in your conversation with your teenager.

Messages you may want to give are:

Nothing you can do will stop me loving you. And I want us to get through this.

Trust is a basic requirement in every relationship. What you've done has damaged my trust in you. You'll have to work hard to earn that trust back.

You made a mistake in judgement. We all make mistakes, but you need to learn from mistakes and move on.

I expect you to take responsibility for what you took.

Today I want to know about anything else you've taken. And I'll expect you to return everything / every penny. If you don't have the money or the items you've stolen, you'll have to earn the full amount and return it anonymously. You can do work at home for £x an hour. Or you can find a job – which would you prefer?

If you want something, let's find a way for you to earn the money to pay for it.

Sometimes people take things that don't belong to them because they feel distant or disconnected. After you've returned anything you've taken, I'd like it if we can find a way to spend some quality time together, and do things that we can both enjoy.

As this is the first time I've spoken to you about taking things, you only need to return what you've taken, and if you can do that anonymously, I'll let you do that.

This has to stop, today!

If you <u>ever</u> take things again, and I hope for your sake you don't, you will not only have to return anything you've taken, you'll have to apologise to that person for taking it. Whether that's someone at school, a shopkeeper, or a relative. I'll come with you, but you'll need to own up to taking it and apologise.

If you take something again that doesn't belong to you, you will also be choosing more serious consequences. It will be your choice. But let me tell you what would happen. If I find money missing from my purse, or I find something in your room that I know doesn't belong to you, I'm going to get the police involved. Getting the police involved can mean inviting a community police officer to your home to talk to your teenager about the consequences of stealing.

You're a good kid. You've made a mistake. But that has to be the end of it. As a parent, it's important for me to help you stop taking things that don't belong to you so it doesn't become a habit that could get you arrested.

I want other people to think you're a good kid. But if you choose to take something from them, I'll know I didn't make enough of an impact on you today to stop you taking things. You <u>earn</u> a good reputation. And if you take things that don't belong to you, you'll damage other people's trust in you. And you need to repair that damage.

I hope in the future that if you see something you want, you find a way to earn the money to buy it. And resist the urge to just take it. Otherwise you risk damaging your reputation. What would your friends or adults you admire think?

I want you to tell me today about everything you've taken. From me, from someone in the family, from a shop or from a friend or *relative. If you don't tell me about something and I find it later on, then I'll have to assume you've taken it <u>after</u> our talk today, and that's when the more serious consequences will kick in. So please don't hide anything from me today. We're going to tackle this today, but it can't carry on.*

10. If the conversation does not go well PLAN AHEAD and decide what you'll do.

It's useful to think about how your teenager will react, and plan how you'll respond.

Justifying the stealing

Your teenager may try to justify the stealing by claiming the money was for a present for you or for a friend. Or for some other very noble purpose. Just remember that no matter what the reason – stealing isn't OK.

"I get why you took the money, but you should have found a way to earn the money. It's <u>never</u> OK to take money without asking."

Getting angry yourself

If *you* start to lose your temper, or feel overwhelmed (perhaps if you discover the extent of their stealing, or if you find out your teenager has been stealing to fund a drug habit) it's OK to take a break and think about what to do next.

"I need a few minutes. Let's take a break and I'll come back shortly."

Your teenager walks off

If your teenager refuses to talk and walks out, you can say:

"You're clearly finding the conversation too difficult to handle at the moment. We'll talk about this later."

And let them leave.

Your teenager lies to you

Many teenagers will feel that if they deny the evidence for long enough, you'll believe them. If your teenager absolutely refuses to admit what they've done, suggest they think about it for half an hour, and that you'll come back to talk to them. Any teenager who is caught up with stealing will probably try to contact someone to back up their story. While you're sorting this out you might like to prevent them using their mobile or electronic devices to contact other people.

If your teenager gets angry or confrontational or aggressive PLAN TO WALK AWAY. Say very calmly:
"I realise you're upset. I get that. I expect you hoped that no one would find out. It's hard when you're caught doing something you shouldn't. Please can you stop shouting? Do you want me to leave you for a few minutes until you're feeling a bit calmer? Please just give me your mobile and laptop before I go."

If your teenager continues to lie to you about where they got the money, or why they have these items in their possession, you can say:
"I'm going to give you a bit of time to think about things before I start making calls to check out your story. I won't be talking with your friends. I will phone their parents. I'm going to give you half an hour to think. And then I'll start making calls. In the meantime, I'd like you to give me your laptop and your mobile."

30 minutes later come back into your teenager's room and say:
"You've had a chance to think now. Are you going to be brave enough now to tell me what really happened? (And wait).

*I **do know** what's happened. Everyone makes mistakes sometimes. What's important is that you own up to a mistake, so you can deal with it and move on.*

I'm just about to phone ...'s parents. I'd rather not involve them, as then they will find out you have taken things and it could damage

your reputation. But I will need to check out what you've told me.
Would you like to change your story?
I will be ringing ...'s parents now. Last chance to admit the truth."
And if necessary, make any calls you need to check out your teenager's story.

Other missing items / money
If other things have disappeared, do not accuse or blame your teenager but ask them if they were responsible. This is the time for them to own up. You absolutely want this to be a confession and not get them justifiably upset by being wrongly accused of something. If it doesn't come up, ask at the end: **"What about the money that went from Jack's money jar? Did you take that too?"**

The main points to remember
1. It's important that you stay completely calm during this conversation. As soon as you lose your temper, the attention will be diverted away from the stealing and on to you. Be ready for your teenager to try to do everything they can to move the attention away from the stealing, and to lie about it. Resolve to stay firm, calm and determined to find out the truth.
2. Do not call your teenager a thief, or keep using the words 'stole' or 'stolen'. Instead use 'taking things without asking'. At the end of the conversation, it is best if your teenager feels that they are a good person who made a mistake. If you try to add to your teenager's guilt with labels and destructive comments, you will damage your teenager's desire to make amends.
3. Do not be tempted to punish your teenager. Although this is a natural reaction, instead insist that your teenager helps with jobs around the house to earn the money to pay back what they've taken from others.
4. Ultimately though, you want your teenager to not steal because they know it's the wrong thing to do: It hurts their

self-image and goes against their own morals and values. They should also want to stop because they value the relationship you have with them *more* than the desire to take things, and they don't want to let you down. If you shout, criticise or impose harsh punishments on your teenager, you will undermine the best reason your teenager has to stop taking things. Initially, your teenager will probably stop because of the fear of what will happen the next time they're caught.

Part 2

Actually having the conversation with your teenager

Write out the conversation you plan to have

When you feel prepared, you will need to talk to your teenager. It would be very useful to read the next section and actually write out the conversation you plan to have with your teenager, so that you are more likely to remember the vital points. This is a very important conversation. If you do this well, you could stop your teenager stealing again, which could be critical for your teenager's future. So it's good to prepare well.

The following conversation is broken down into sections to reflect different scenarios. Read the examples then adapt them to suit your own circumstances, and to reflect the language you'd normally use.

Starting the conversation

Once you have evidence that your teenager is stealing, you can plan to have the conversation to tackle it. It's good to put the item(s), money or evidence your teenager has stolen on the table and say: 'We need to talk!'

"I want to talk to you about something serious. Is now a good time? I found £40 missing from my purse this morning. And I found THIS under your mattress. I'm not going to ask how it got there. I know you took it. I'd prefer you not to try to make up any stories about why there is money under your mattress.
It can be hard when someone finds out that you've been taking things. I imagine you hoped I wouldn't find out.
What you were going to use the money for?"

If your teenager denies taking it say: *"You're not telling me the truth. Have a think for a moment. And then we'll see if you're brave enough to tell me what really happened.*

When people take things that don't belong to them, they don't want to get caught. So they sometimes lie to cover it up. You may be trying to think of an explanation I'll believe for the money being there. If you do that, everything gets complicated, because you'll try to involve other people. But I'm asking you to tell the truth now."

Find out if your teenager has taken anything else

Ask your teenager directly if they've stolen anything else. And explain why you think this may have happened before. Recognise they've probably been worried about being found out. Sometimes they may find it easier to write down things they've taken.

If your teenager asks what is going to happen, tell them that this time they'll only need to return what they've stolen, and do 10-15 hours of work for free to make up for the distress they've caused. However, if they ever do it again, (or you find something they've taken that they haven't admitted to at a later date) they will need to own up and apologise. And you will involve the police.

If your teenager confesses to taking anything else, ask your teenager to fetch the item, name the amount of money they've stolen, or if they no longer have the item, to say how much they think the item was worth.

Confiscate any money or items that have been stolen. Remove any game from their computer that was downloaded without permission. It's important not to allow them to benefit from anything they've taken.

"What else have you taken? (If they deny they've stolen before, press the issue.)

"I think it's unlikely that that's true. £40 is a lot of money to take. It's rare to be caught the first time. Often when people start taking

things, and aren't caught straight away, it can become a bit of a habit. So what else have you taken before this?

You've probably been worried about taking things and what would happen if you were caught. You're normally so good. It can't have felt good taking things that don't belong to you. You may even have wanted to stop, but it became a habit.

Today we're going to get it sorted. But I need you to be honest with me now.

I'm going to give you a sheet of paper and a pen. I'd like you to write down everything you've taken without asking. I'll give you ten minutes. And I'll come back in and then we'll go through the list.

I'm giving you a chance to own up now. I know you're not a bad person. We'll get this sorted, but I want to know if there's anything else. So please write down anything else you've taken.

If you don't admit to taking something now, and later on I find something that doesn't belong to you, I'll have to assume that you've taken it since our conversation today, and get the police involved. I don't want to involve the police today, to give you a chance to stop taking things that don't belong to you. However, if you take anything in the future, it would mean you can't stop yourself.

I'd rather not involve the police, but I'll do what's necessary to help you to stop. If you don't want me to involve the police for something you've already taken, and haven't told me about, now is your chance to come clean."

When your teenager has written their list, go through it and ask:
"Can you go and fetch that?"
If they haven't still got it:
"How much was it worth?"

Talk about your expectations

As mentioned earlier, do not call your teenager names (thief, shoplifter, etc.) Although you can tell them how this has made you feel, (I feel...), try to say things in a neutral way. If you criticise, blame, judge and label your teenager, they will not feel safe owning up. If you threaten harsh punishments they won't feel able to tell you about things they've taken. You can explain that losing your trust is one of the natural consequences of their actions, but tell them you expect them to be honest and trustworthy.

"Relationships are built on trust. I realise that you felt it was OK to take my money. But this means that in the future if I have less money in my purse than I think I should have, or something goes missing at home I'll wonder if you've taken it. You'll be the first person I suspect.

I'll worry you might decide to take something else, from a shop or from someone we know. I'll start to check my money more carefully. And I won't be able to fully relax, knowing that you've taken my money once. When I'm with you, there will be that nagging doubt that perhaps you'll do it again.

That's the consequence of taking things. It will take a long time to rebuild the trust I used to feel in you. If you want people to trust you, you earn their trust.

I feel really hurt and disappointed that you chose to take money from me."

"I expect this to stop today. It's not OK to take things that don't belong to you.

From now on I want you to be honest and trustworthy. And to earn money if you want to buy anything.

If you're caught taking things that don't belong to you, you'll lose the respect from people who trust you – teachers, adults you like friends and members of the family.

People won't trust you in the future. It might ruin your reputation and could get you a criminal record.

You're not a bad person. What you did was a mistake, but it's a mistake that needs to stop today."

Expect your teenager to make amends

You can ask your teenager what they think would be a suitable consequence. If they have just taken the money from your purse, you can talk about how you'll tackle that. But they should *also* have to do some jobs at home, *for free*, to help them make up for the distress that they've caused and help repair the hurt. This is important, as your teenager has done something that damaged your relationship. So 'making amends' is important for their inner well-being and sense of justice. Perhaps 10 or 15 hours of jobs for free.

What do you think would be a good way to make up for taking the money?
When you take things from someone – in order to make up for it – you need to say sorry and admit that you did something wrong. You need to pay them back – every penny – with money from savings, by selling your stuff, or by doing jobs around the home. And you need to do something nice for them on top of that to show you're really sorry. For me, that will be doing jobs that will help everyone in the family.
When you've done something that hurts and upsets others, it's important to repair the damage by doing something to say sorry. I'd like you to do 15 hours of jobs – for free – to make up for your mistake.
Here's a list of jobs that you could do. (See list below). *You can choose which jobs you'd like to do from the list.*
Do you think you could manage one hour a day? That's 15 hours that you'll work without being paid.
Then you can carry on earning at £X an hour to pay back the money you've taken.

If your teenager has taken a lot of money ask if they would prefer to pay back *half* the amount by taking it out of their savings. They should earn the rest by doing jobs around the house.

When all the money has been repaid, you can carry on after that to earn money for the things you want.

As you don't still have Y (whatever your teenager has taken) in your possession, you can earn the money to replace it, and either buy a new one, and send it back to the person you took it from, or send an anonymous note with the money explaining that you are sending the money to replace the item.

Explain what the consequences will be, both now and in the future.

Explain to your teenager that this time, they just need to return what they've stolen. If they have taken money, insist they earn the money doing jobs at home so they can repay it. Choose an amount which is below the 'minimum wage' and that you can afford. If you can't afford to pay for jobs, your teenager will need to brainstorm other ways they can earn the money. If the sum taken is a large amount then allow them to take some of the money out of their savings. I would suggest no more than half of the money can be repaid through taking money out of savings – if they have that amount. Doing jobs is a very important way to repair the damage and learn how to earn money! Make sure your teenager understands that next time they'll have to confess and apologise to anyone they've taken something from as well. And that you will involve the police.

"This time I'm not going to ask you to own up to everyone you've taken things from.
You probably want to keep your good reputation and for other people to think well of you. So I'm just going to ask you to find a way to return things.

If you've spent money you've taken, or no longer have what you took, then you can earn the money to buy it and replace it by finding a paid job or doing jobs around the house. I'll give you an hourly rate of £x.

If it's possible to return things anonymously, then you can do that this time.

If I ever catch you taking things again, you'll have to return what you've taken. And own up to the person you've taken it from.

That's because if you take things again, then you know you will be choosing that as a consequence. Returning what you've taken, owning up and apologising.

At that point, I'll probably contact the police. Because it would mean that having our conversation today won't have persuaded you to stop taking things. It's hard to break a habit. But if you can't stop yourself, it may be good to get some outside help.

I still love you very much. I'm sad that you took money without asking. It is going to take a while for me to trust you again. And you'll need to earn that trust. But I know you'll learn from this."

If you can, find out why your teenager has been stealing

If you can, try to get to the bottom of why they stole something. But remember to stay calm, avoid being judgemental, and try to react with empathy and understanding.

"I know you know it was the wrong thing to do. Can you tell me why you took the money? Usually when teenagers take things from someone they love they're feeling bad about something. Is there any reason that you can think of?"

If your teenager talks about problems or difficulties, *do not let your teenager off the consequences,* but say: *"Thank you for telling me that. It's ok to feel fed up / jealous / annoyed. Later on we'll sit down and see if we can sort out how to deal with that."*

What if you found a whole stash of things that have been stolen?

Confront your teenager with the evidence. Put the items on the table in front of you. But remember to try to help your teenager feel that they are a good person who made a mistake, not a bad person.

"I've noticed a few things going missing recently, and when I was in your room I checked on top of your wardrobe and found these! Here's a computer game, a whole lot of money and a couple of DVDs that I've never seen before.

I know you know that it was wrong to take things without asking. You must have been feeling bad about it, even though you were probably justifying it to yourself. You knew it was wrong. Because you're normally so good, I'm guessing you've been feeling guilty about taking things. Well now it's out in the open, we need to deal with it."

If your teenager tries to divert attention away from them.

If your teenager gets angry that you've been 'snooping' in their room, don't allow yourself to be distracted.

"I realise you feel angry that I was in your room. I get that. You'd like to feel your room is private. And getting angry at me is a good way to steer the attention away from the things you took. However, privacy is something you <u>earn</u>. It's not a right. Right now we're going to discuss the items I found. Later on we can talk about how you earn privacy."

What if your teenager has been shoplifting, and you want them to return the item?

If this is the first time you have caught your teenager shoplifting, you may allow them to wrap the item up and pay the postage to return the item to the shop.

However, if this is the second time, or you feel that it's important for your teenager to face the consequences, let your teenager know they'll need to return the items to the shop or pay for them. Let them know that you won't protect them from the consequences. And then plan how and when you'll return with them to the shop.

"Sam, I was upset to find this PlayStation game in your wardrobe. I know you were looking at this game in the shop earlier today. So you brought it home without paying for it. And now we need to talk about how you're going to return it.
I'm not going to protect you from the consequences. We need to go back to the shop. You need to return it and apologise to the manager."

1. Call the shop anonymously and ask to talk to the manager. Ask what would happen if you brought a teenager to the shop to return something they'd taken. If the shop's policy is to prosecute first time offenders, you may need to reconsider taking your teenager in (and return the item by post).
2. If the shop manager agrees not to prosecute, agree a time when you'll bring your teenager in. Ask the manager to talk to your teenager about the seriousness of stealing, security cameras, and the cost of shoplifting to the retailer.
3. Warn your teenager beforehand that they may hear things they don't like, but they need to listen, acknowledge what is being said and apologise. Be aware that the shop manager may not be as gentle as you are!
4. At the agreed time, take your teenager in to see the manager to return or pay for the items.
5. Afterwards, tell your teenager you're pleased that they took responsibility for what they did, and that you're sure they won't make the same mistake again. Make sure you tell your teenager you love them and forgive them, and that the matter is now over.

Jobs your teenager can do to make amends

It is imperative that your teenager pays back every penny of the money that they stole, or the equivalent value of items they stole. Work out what jobs your teenager can do, and offer them the going rate of pay for a teenager. Look at the minimum wage and deduct a bit to account for your teenager's age.

If you can't afford to pay your teenager to work at home, you could also agree a set rate with neighbours and family for jobs your teenager can do. Other people don't have to know where the money is going as your teenager will want to preserve their reputation as a good kid. And you don't need to affect that – unless your teenager has stolen anything from the neighbours or friends!

If your teenager is old enough to do paid work, then they can give you a percentage of their earnings. You can discuss with them whether you'll take 50%, 75% or 100% until the debt is paid.

Please note: don't ever pay a teenager for clearing up their own mess, doing homework or keeping their room tidy. These are things your teenager should be doing for themselves, and don't ever pay for a job that's badly done.

Suitable jobs a teenager can do:
Clean surfaces of downstairs rooms
Dust
Vacuum
Sweep the floor
Mop the floor
Wash walls, skirting boards and white-painted woodwork
Clean toilets / bathrooms
Clean the kitchen
Clean the oven
Sort books and magazines
Change sheets / bedcovers

Empty wastebaskets
Take out bins
Weed the garden
Rake leaves
Mow the lawn
Water the flowers
Set the table
Unload and load the dishwasher
Wash the dishes
Clear up after a meal
Wash table and counter-tops after meals
Sort laundry
Wash, dry and fold laundry and put clothes away
Iron clothes
Sew on buttons
Mend clothes
Do the family's grocery shopping
Put away groceries
Make breakfast
Make packed lunches
Peel vegetables
Help prepare meals with you
Cook simple meals for the whole family
Take a pet for a walk
Clean pet area / Care for pets
Wash windows
Wash the car
Babysit younger siblings
Babysit for friends or relatives (if old enough)

After everything is repaid, your teenager should continue doing regular jobs or chores for 'love' just because they're part of a family. After they have completed their 'regular jobs', your teenager can earn money to buy things they want or need by doing additional jobs.

Part 3:

Repairing the relationship

When your teenager is doing regular jobs to pay back the money for things they've taken, you should find that they start to take on a more mature attitude. It is preferable for you to do the chores together. While you're working together don't talk about the stealing, but chat about anything that will interest them: their lives, interests, friends, schoolwork, thoughts and attitudes towards things. When you work alongside your teenager, specifically to rebuild the relationship, there are some useful things you can do that help build a closer bond between you.

When working alongside your teenager remember these three guidelines:
- Don't be cross, grumpy or angry
- Don't criticise or judge
- Don't give advice

So what can you do?
- Make an effort to be friendly and fun. Always be determined to stay calm, and make sure that if your teenager says or does something that causes you to feel angry or annoyed you deliberately stop yourself from losing it.
- Listen and explore why your teenager thinks certain things. Accept their thoughts and views. And don't share your own attitudes and opinions *unless they ask you*. If you do share your own attitudes and opinions don't expect your teenager to agree with you.
- Rather than telling your teenager what to do, if your teenager shares a problem, or has a difficulty, *ask your teenager* how they think they'll handle it. What options can they think of? And perhaps do a problem solving exercise to help them sort it out.

These are difficult guidelines to follow. But there is a very good reason for following them. There's a strong likelihood that your teenager doesn't see much of your happy, fun side anymore. There's a chance that your teenager feels you don't ever really listen to them: they actually feel criticised and judged a lot of the time. They may have decided that in your eyes they can't do anything right, that they don't dare to talk to you about their beliefs or thoughts that differ from your own. And it's also possible they think that every time they talk to you, you end up telling them what to do.

Doing the chores alongside your teenager as they work to pay back for things they've taken gives you an opportunity to change what's going on between you and your teenager. Follow these guidelines to repair the relationship and you stand the best chance of building a closer bond with your teenager.

When your teenager has completed the jobs required to pay back for items or money they've taken, try to spend at least 15 minutes a day listening and communicating with your teenager using these guidelines. If your son or daughter has quality time with you every day, you will find you feel closer to your teenager and any rifts between you, caused by the stealing, will be quicker to heal. Good times to talk are in the car, when you're walking together or when you're doing a shared task. Hugs or just touching an arm or shoulder are also important ways to reconnect with your teenager.

Problem solving

If your teenager needs to earn more money to pay you back or buy things they want, brainstorm ideas to help them think how they could earn that money:
- Write the issue at the top of the page. Something like 'Ellie wants to earn money to pay for clothes'.
- Then ask your teenager to think of as many possible ways they could earn the money. Try to get your teenager to come up with

10-15 ideas. Make sure you write down all their ideas – even the silly or ridiculous ones! This process helps open up the creative part of a teenager's brain.

- If you have any ideas of your own, <u>ask</u> if you can add them at the end.
- Cross off any ideas that are illegal, impossible or just not practical!
- Ask your teenager to choose which ideas he or she wants to try first.

The commitment conversation

When you feel your teenager is ready, it would be good to talk to your teenager about stealing and try to make sure that your teenager is committed to stop taking things.

Explain that ANY future stealing – *no matter how small* – will result in 4 consequences. Your teenager will need to:
1.   Return anything they've taken.
2.   Apologise to the person they took it from.
3.   Do 15 hours of jobs at home – with no payment – to make amends.
4.   Talk with a police officer about stealing.

It is very important you explain this to your teenager, so they are absolutely certain of the results of stealing anything else. And you will need to be prepared to follow through.

Once you have explained this, to be sure your teenager understands and is committed to stop the stealing, ask your teenager questions *rather* than telling them what to do.

Good questions to ask are:
- **How are you feeling about the things you took now?**
- **What have you learned from doing the jobs to make amends?**
- **Do you think you'll be tempted to take things again?**

- **What do you think will be the hardest temptation to resist?**
- **How will you handle that?**
- **What are the risks if you do take something that doesn't belong to you in the future?** (Loss of respect and trust from other people, possible criminal charges, etc.)
- **What consequences will you be choosing if you do steal something?** (Return everything that was taken, apologise, 15 hours of jobs, talk to police.)
- **Does it matter how small the item is that you take?** (No, even if the item is *tiny*, you will still be choosing the 4 consequences.)
- _**Can**_ **you stop yourself taking things that aren't yours?**
- _**Will**_ **you stop taking things that don't belong to you?**

It would be good to finish the conversation with a hug, or a pat on the back and some reassurance:
"I love you so much. Everyone makes mistakes, but I really think you've learned from this, and we can put it behind us now."

If your teenager steals a second time

If after having your conversation, your teenager takes something else that doesn't belong to them, then it's important to stick to your guns and follow through with the consequences you've threatened.

You will need to be 100% sure that your teenager has stolen the item or money. Remember, however, that your teenager will be much more likely to lie to you if they know which consequences will follow.

These will be hard for you as a parent to enforce. But your teenager needs you to be firm. If they have stolen something again, they will have been forewarned and will effectively have chosen these consequences.

1. Returning the item or money

You will need to insist your teenager returns the item to the person they took it from.

2. A good apology

Your teenager will need to apologise to the person they've taken something from. A good apology has four parts. Your teenager needs to:

- Say: **"I'm sorry."**
- Admit that what they did that was wrong and also take responsibility for what they did. They should not deflect the blame, implicate others, or try to justify their actions. **"I know it was wrong to take it. I wasn't really thinking clearly. It was a stupid thing to do."**
- Find a way to make up for what they did. Perhaps say: **"I'm returning the money (or item) I took. Is there any other way I can make it up to you?"** They should be prepared to do what the other person asks them to do.
- And ask: **"Am I forgiven?"** or **"Will you forgive me?"**

Teenagers learn by example. It is best if they see *you* apologising, to others and to them so they know how it feels to be on the receiving end of an honest apology. When you give your teenager a genuine apology, they will internalise its value rather than just see it as a 'technique' or something that *they* should do, but not something a *parent* has to do.

Apologising is hard. There are always two sides to a story, and inevitably there is bad feeling when a teenager has stolen something. A genuine 'sorry' may make your teenager feel vulnerable, but in fact it takes a lot of courage to be able to apologise.

3. 15 hours of jobs

Arrange which jobs your teenager will do for 15 hours without payment, and exactly when they will do them. This is to make up for the damage they have done to your trust, and the hurt they've caused by stealing again.

4. Talk to the police

Ring the local police, and ask if there is an officer who works in the community or with young offenders. Explain that your teenager has stolen in the past, and that you haven't been able to stop them. Say you are trying to be a responsible parent by asking the police for help to stop your teenager stealing.

Ask if you can get a police officer to talk with your teenager about the consequences of stealing, and tell your teenager stories of young people getting criminal convictions. Sometimes police officers can be more judgemental or aggressive than parents would like. While this is hard to observe, the impact on your teenager may be exactly the shock your teenager needs to change.

Do not prosecute your teenager. Or press criminal charges.

These consequences are hard to enforce, and hard for your teenager to experience, but will help your teenager to resist the impulse to steal in the future.

What if your teenager won't return stolen money or goods? Or refuses to work to pay back the value of the things they've taken?

No teenager will want to return what they've taken. It will be one of the hardest things they have ever had to do. Try to do everything you can to help your teenager to understand why they need to apologise and return stolen property, and why they need to earn the money to pay people back. Empathise with how hard it is, but insist it's the right way to repair the damage.

If your teenager still won't agree, there are two options: involve the police or withdraw what you normally do for your teenager. Many parents don't feel they hold any cards but you probably do a lot for your teenager. You can go on strike, and generally make life difficult for them.

Please don't take the following list out of context. Going on strike is only an option when a teenager is defiant or aggressive towards you, and won't take responsibility for earning the money or returning items they've stolen. Going on strike should only be used when you have no other way of helping your teenager learn. And you should *never lose your temper or shout or get angry when using it*. When you are refusing to do things for your teenager you say it in a calm loving way, and tell your teenager that when they do what you ask and return what they've taken you'll be happy to resume doing things for them.

You may need to confiscate things that belong to you that your teenager uses. You can refuse to cook, clean, shop or give lifts to your teenager (apart from to and from school if they can't get to school by walking or taking public transport). You can provide only basic, value food. No treats or luxuries! You can cancel their phone contract, lock your money away and stop giving them *any* money.

You can remove video game consoles, laptops and so on, from your home on the basis that a teenager should earn 'screen time' with good behaviour. All the while you should try to stay totally calm. Try NEVER to lose your temper. Empathise with how hard this is for your teenager. Understand that they are angry. But keep insisting that 'normal service will be resumed' when your teenager returns stolen goods and apologises for stealing.

If your teenager agrees to return stolen goods, but has spent the money they stole, then agree a work schedule for them to earn the money. And agree which privileges they can earn for good behaviour. Do not pay the money in advance. Make sure they earn it. And they can watch the total go up. Agree which jobs they can do (over and above their regular chores) and agree an hourly rate. If you can, it is best to work alongside your teenager, and use the time to reconnect. While you do the jobs together DON'T mention the stealing. Use the time to rebuild your relationship with them. And spend time chatting about anything your teenager is interested in, but NOT their bad behaviour.

Do not use 'going on strike' to *punish* your teenager. Going on strike should only to be used if your teenager refuses to take responsibility for the stealing and return the stolen goods. You may feel awful having to go through this strategy. But explain firmly and kindly to your teenager that you have to do this, as a good parent, to help them learn from their mistake and make amends. Explain you want to do everything in your power to get them to stop stealing, and if this is what it takes, then that's what you'll do. Always bear in mind what the long-term consequences will be if they *don't* stop stealing (e.g. possible criminal prosecutions or prison) and tell them that you wouldn't forgive yourself if you didn't do everything in your power to help them stop stealing now.

If, after a while, your teenager is doing a good amount of work, you may negotiate which privileges can be reinstated. Your teenager may be desperate to keep a bit of the money they earn to pay for things. Do not agree to anything you're not happy with. But gradually you can soften your approach if your teenager is working hard to repay the stolen money. However, never be tempted to let them off without earning the *full* amount back. Be absolutely firm on this one.

What if your teenager won't stop stealing?

If your teenager continues to steal, it's important to keep all valuables and money locked away.

Call in a community police officer to talk to your son or daughter about the impact of stealing and what the consequences would be if your teenager was arrested for stealing. Make sure your teenager is in absolutely no doubt that you *will* call the police if anything goes missing again.

If valuable belongings or a large amount of money goes missing, you may choose to report the theft to the police. You will need to consider carefully whether to pursue criminal charges. In general, this is not a good course of action. But if the stealing is so entrenched, you may have to decide: would you rather *you* called the police on your teenager or that they were arrested for stealing outside the home?

Sometimes, there is a breakdown in the relationship that cannot be rectified while a teenager is living at home. Once your teenager is over the age of 16, there are options for them to move out of the family home. No family should be subjected to a teenager who continues to steal from them despite all their efforts to help them stop. Occasionally it helps if a teenager can move out of the family home. But always bear in mind, ***your relationship with your teenager is still more important than anything***. If your teenager moves out, it is still good to meet up with them and try to have the best relationship you can with them. If you agree to them returning to the family home, let them know that if your teenager *ever* steals from you again they will have to leave again.

Long-term strategies to prevent future stealing

In the long term, how can you reduce the likelihood of your teenager stealing again?

Encourage your teenager to take on jobs at home. One of the most important things you can do to help your teenager stop their stealing habit is to encourage them to contribute to family life. It's important to agree with your teenager which jobs they will do 'for love' and which they can do to earn money. Stealing from others comes from an underlying attitude of entitlement and helping out at home is essential if your teenager is to lose the false belief that they are 'entitled' to things that belong to others. Taking on a small part -time job, outside the home, may also help.

Encourage participation in worthwhile activities. You can also encourage them to do extra-curricular activities. In the UK, teenagers can do a 'Duke of Edinburgh' award. Or your teenager could get engaged in volunteering, scouts, sports or music — something that could help boost their self-esteem.

Support good friendships. It's also good to encourage your teenager to mix with friends that you feel are good for them. Allow these friends into your home and encourage those friendships to blossom. Try to spend some time with your teenager's friends and engage with them.

Establish a communication channel. Sometimes teenagers find it hard to share their problems or difficulties with parents. Talk to your teenager and explain that they can talk to you about what is going on and establish a way to make it safe, where you won't lose your temper. Perhaps have a code word for when they need to have an important conversation with you.

Lead by example If your teenager has been stealing, it's very important that you make sure honesty and trust are qualities that you not only demonstrate through your actions, but also that you talk openly about them. You may be upset and angry about your teenager's stealing but try to make sure you always act honestly by:

- Correcting the mistake if someone in a shop or restaurant gives you too much change.
- Making sure you never take stationery or items from work for your own personal use.
- Making sure you never take cutlery from a restaurant or canteen.

It's good to look at where you may have given your teenager inconsistent messages about being trustworthy. Try to be as honest as you can when dealing with others in the future.

Don't leave money around. That is just putting temptation in your teenager's path. Keep your money in a safe place, and keep a proper account of it, so you'd know if any went missing. If you're worried, mark any bank notes in your purse, so you would know the money was from your purse if you found it in your teenager's possession.

Have clear rules. Make sure your teenager knows the rules about taking things without asking. They should know exactly which consequences they'll be choosing if they decide to take things from other people. But tell your teenager you never expect to have to use the consequences you've outlined.

Allow your teenager to earn money. If you give pocket money or an allowance, try to make it a small amount. Make sure your teenager knows how to earn money by doing jobs for you or others.

Discuss stealing, honesty and trust. Regularly bring up and discuss stories you have heard from the news or TV programmes where stealing has been an issue.

Treat your children fairly. Try not to have favourites or stir up competition. Help each of your children feel loved, important and accepted in the home. Stealing is more likely to happen when a teenager feels that other children are favoured, openly admired or given preferential treatment, or if they don't feel valued.

A good father figure / male role model. Researchers have found that teenagers are less likely to steal if they have a firm but fair father figure. If your teenager doesn't have a good dad around, try to enlist the help of a man you respect, who can take an interest in your teenager and spend time with them to listen, motivate and guide them. Someone who can act as a role model and mentor.

Have clear expectations. Make sure your teenager knows you expect them to be honest and trustworthy and to respect other people's possessions. Try to steer them onto the right path. Impress on your teenager that you never expect them to steal again.

Finally...

You should be able to stop your teenager's stealing habit when you prepare what to say before you tackle the stealing, when you are consistent and firm about the consequences, and when you work to repair the relationship with your teenager.

Well done for taking the time to tackle this difficult issue. Good luck in helping your teenager to understand the value of being honest and trustworthy, and congratulations on reading this guide to help your teenager develop the morals and values they'll need to become decent, moral adults in the future.

To your parenting success!
Elizabeth

About the Author

Elizabeth O'Shea lives with her husband, Maurice, in Horsham, in the UK. Her children, Katie, George, Sophie and Emily are now young adults, so Elizabeth has guided four children through their teenage years.

Elizabeth did a degree in Nursing at Kings College, London and became a Nursing Sister at Dulwich hospital. She took a career break to raise her children, and taught Positively Parenting classes in 2000. She returned to nursing, helping nurses back into the NHS. She worked for over five years for Home-Start and then helped 'parents-to-be' to break the cycle of abuse and neglect they had suffered in the past. Elizabeth also trained to run four different types of parenting courses.

In 2011 Elizabeth set up her own business, Parent 4 Success. She now regularly appears as a parenting expert on a variety of news channels, such as Sky News and BBC Breakfast, contributing to national news stories. She was featured in the Guardian Weekend magazine with other 'top negotiators' showing parents how to negotiate with children.

Elizabeth mainly works with parents either face-to-face or on Skype, to help them manage issues with their children's behaviour. These issues include sleeping problems, aggression, homework, bullying, friendship issues, sibling rivalry, difficult teenagers, children going off the rails, children coping with divorce or working parents, and of course, teenagers stealing. Elizabeth also runs parenting courses and workshops in schools and is invited as a speaker to talk to parents and professionals about parenting issues.

You can read Elizabeth's parenting blogs on her website www.parent4success.com which attracts thousands of visitors each month.

In her spare time, Elizabeth reads novels and has belonged to the same book group for over 20 years. She also enjoys photography and spending time with her family.

Do you need specialist help?

All the information in this guide is written to help you to stop your teenager stealing. However, stealing may be a symptom of a teenager who is feeling disconnected and resentful.

Elizabeth works with many families to help them repair the relationship with their teenagers and get things back on track, where both parents and teenagers feel respected and valued in their own homes.

Please feel free to call Elizabeth (in confidence) to discuss whether working with her in the future would help you and your family. And establish a better bond with your teenager.

Nothing can prepare you for life with a teenager, and sometimes every parent needs a bit of extra help. But please rest assured, you are not alone. There is help. There are solutions. And Elizabeth would love to help you get the relationship you want and deserve with your teenager.

If you're ready to tackle the stealing and invest in repairing your relationship with your teenager, call Elizabeth on 01403 839683, or go to www.parent4success.com and click on 'Contact Elizabeth'.

Printed in Great Britain
by Amazon